DINO DUEL

ALLOSAURUS VS. STEGOSAURUS

Prehistoric Showdown

Tom Jackson

Lerner Publications ◆ Minneapolis

Lerner Publications Company
An imprint of Lerner Publishing Group, Inc.
241 First Avenue North
Minneapolis, MN 55401 USA

For reading levels and more information, look up this title at www.lernerbooks.com.

Main body text set in Aptifer Sans LT Pro.
Typeface provided by Linotype.

Library of Congress Cataloging-in-Publication Data

Names: Jackson, Tom, 1972–author
Title: Allosaurus vs. stegosaurus : prehistoric showdown / Tom Jackson.
Other titles: Allosaurus versus stegosaurus
Description: Minneapolis : Lerner Publications, [2026] | Series: Dino duel | Includes bibliographical references and index. | Audience term: juvenile | Audience term: juvenile | Audience: Ages 8–11 Lerner Publications | Audience: Grades 4–6 Lerner Publications | Summary: "The allosaurus can run fast and has sharp claws and teeth. But the stegosaurus is much heavier, with thick skin and bone plates along its back. Readers learn about these dinosaurs' traits, and who would win in a fight"—Provided by publisher.
Identifiers: LCCN 2024044001 (print) | LCCN 2024044002 (ebook) | ISBN 9798765669228 (lib. bdg.) | ISBN 9798765683897 (pbk.) | ISBN 9798765676615 (epub)
Subjects: LCSH: Allosaurus—Juvenile literature | Stegosaurus—Juvenile literature
Classification: LCC QE862.S3 J328 2026 (print) | LCC QE862.S3 (ebook) | DDC 567.912—dc23/eng/20250214

LC record available at https://lccn.loc.gov/2024044001
LC ebook record available at https://lccn.loc.gov/2024044002

Manufactured in the United States of America
1 – CG – 7/15/25

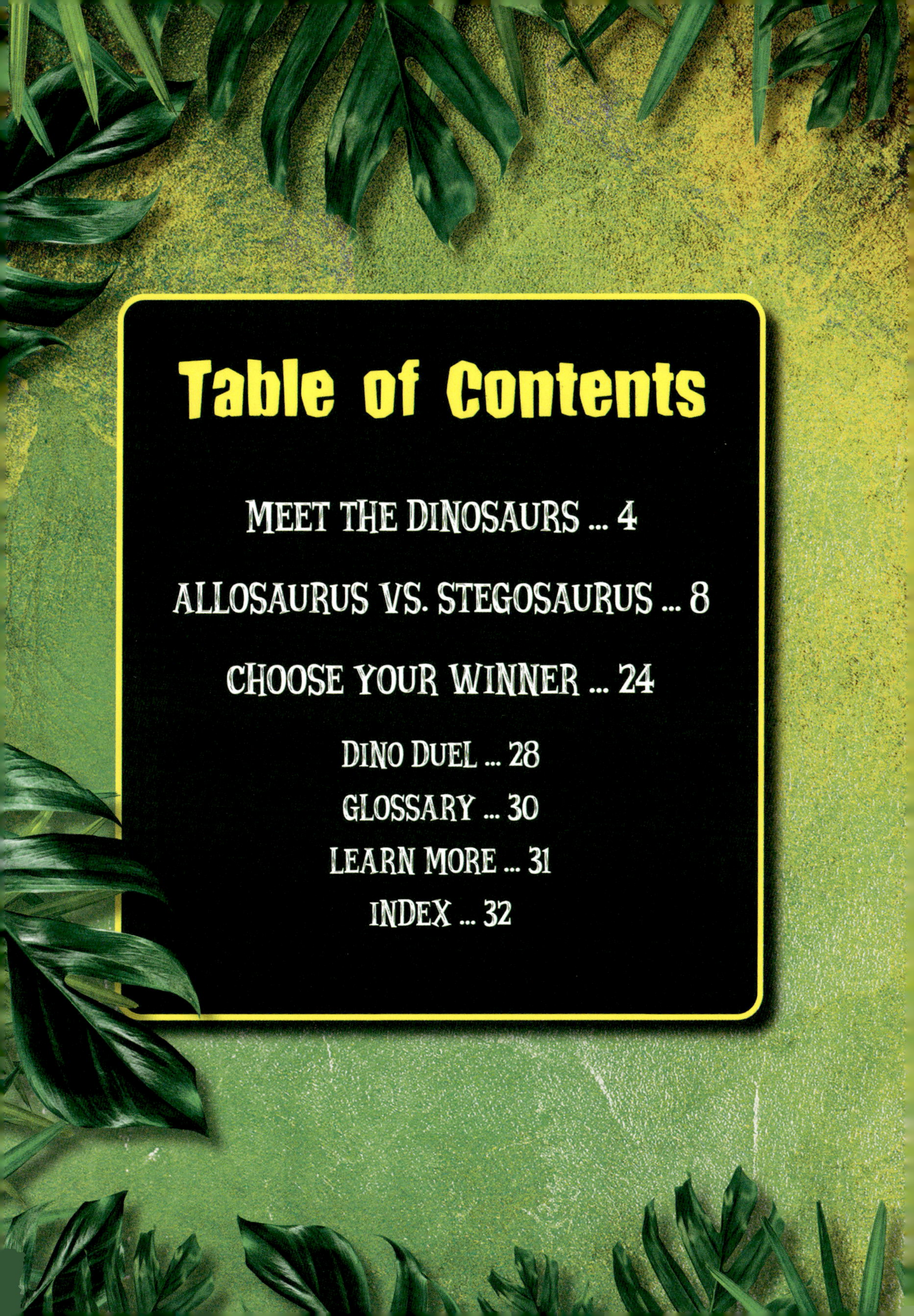

Table of Contents

The stegosaurus senses danger!

A stegosaurus is walking in the warm sunlight between tall trees. The huge dinosaur is hungry and searching for its next meal. It only eats plants so it must look for food all day long. It has found a patch of small leafy ferns to eat. The dinosaur lowers its head to take a bite. But wait! What's that noise?

Two nearby allosauruses are hungry as well. They have been watching the stegosaurus for some time. They stay hidden behind trees and bushes as they creep closer and closer. The two hunters are ready to attack. It is now or never.

Both dinosaurs lived in what is now North America.

Crash! The stegosaurus turns its head in time to see the two allosaurus attackers charge out into the open. One of the allosauruses plunges its teeth into the stegosaurus's back leg. The other tries to bite the big stegosaurus's neck, but the flat plates there get in the way.

The stegosaurus can fight back. It has protective plates running down its back and is much heavier than its attackers. It swings its thick tail covered in long spikes toward its predators. The allosauruses take a step back. The fight for survival has started. Who will win?

DINO STATS

Allosaurus

Weight: 1.7 tons (1.5 t)
Length: 30 feet (9 m)
Main weapons: Hooked teeth, sharp claws, fast running speed

Stegosaurus

Weight: 6 tons (5.4 t)
Length: 30 feet (9 m)
Main weapons: Spiked tail, bone plates along back, thick skin

ALLOSAURUS VS. STEGOSAURUS

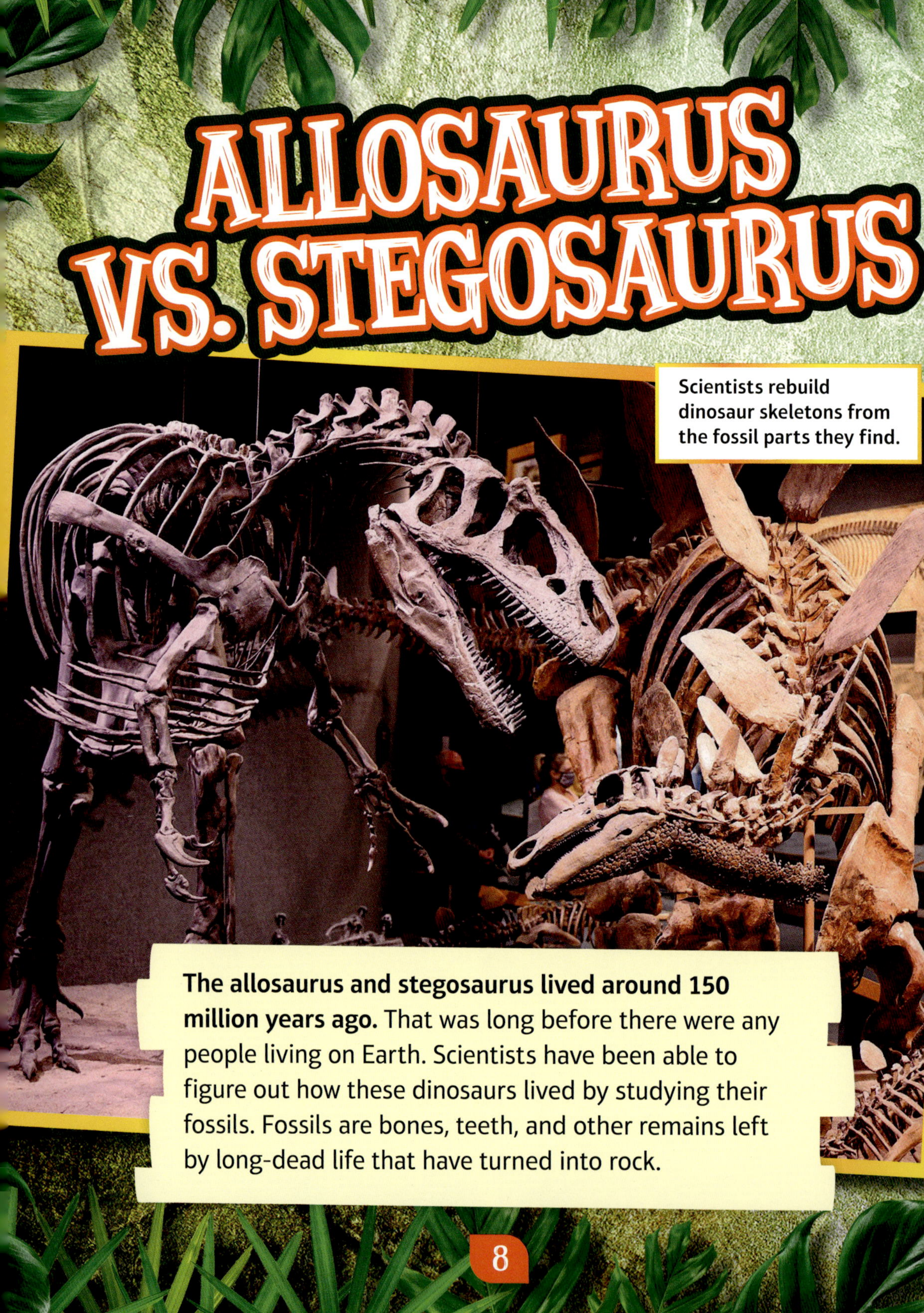

Scientists rebuild dinosaur skeletons from the fossil parts they find.

The allosaurus and stegosaurus lived around 150 million years ago. That was long before there were any people living on Earth. Scientists have been able to figure out how these dinosaurs lived by studying their fossils. Fossils are bones, teeth, and other remains left by long-dead life that have turned into rock.

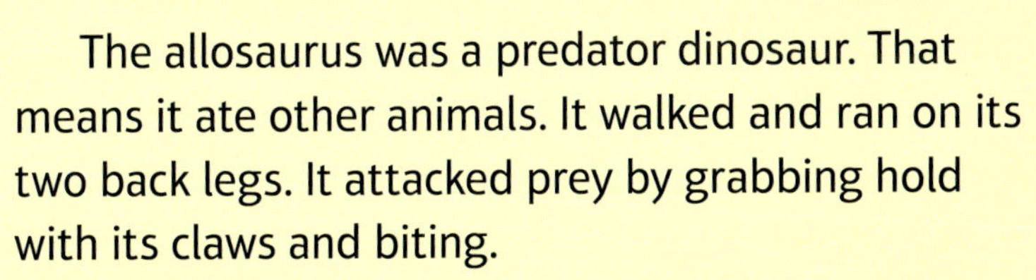

The allosaurus was a predator dinosaur. That means it ate other animals. It walked and ran on its two back legs. It attacked prey by grabbing hold with its claws and biting.

The stegosaurus was a plant-eating dinosaur. It had tall plates of bone standing up in a row on its back. Some experts think these helped the dinosaur keep warm and protect against predators.

A fossil hunter digs out a dinosaur skeleton from rocks.

Size Up

Both these dinosaurs were of a medium size. They were both around the same length, about as long as a school bus. However, the stegosaurus was much heavier than the allosaurus. The stegosaurus had a wide barrel-shaped body, while the allosaurus was more slender.

Both the dinosaurs had long tails. Allosauruses' tails made up about half of their whole body length. They had a thick neck with a big head. Stegosauruses' tails were only a third of their body, but they also had a long neck that could move with ease.

Allosauruses grew very fast. At the age of three, they weighed around 60 pounds (27 kg). By the age of fifteen they were full-size and fifty-five times heavier!

Heads Together

One of the biggest differences between these two dinosaurs was the size of their heads. A fully grown allosaurus's head was almost 3 feet (90 cm) long. That is the width of a single bed. An allosaurus's teeth were quite small though. Each one was about 2 inches (6 cm) long, which is as long as a pinky finger. However, each of their thirty teeth was hooked with a sharp tip!

Stegosauruses had a small skull compared to the rest of their body. It was 16 inches (40 cm) long. There were no teeth at the front, just a hard shape similar to a bird's beak. The teeth farther back were very small.

An allosaurus had two crests of bone on the top of its skull. The crests may have been brightly colored. These colors would have showed off how healthy and tough the dinosaur was.

Feeding Time

Stegosauruses ate small, leafy plants that grew close to the ground. They had a flexible neck made up of thirteen bones. This is one of the highest numbers of neck bones of any dinosaur. The human neck has only seven bones in it. Stegosauruses used their neck to reach down to the ground. They snipped off leaves with their beak-like mouth. Then the dinosaur would chew them up with their back teeth. Next the leaves went into their huge stomach. Inside, the food was digested very slowly.

Stegosauruses were often on the move looking for new plants to eat.

A stegosaurus did not chew its food much. Instead it swallowed small stones. These rubbed together inside the stomach, grinding up the food inside into a mush.

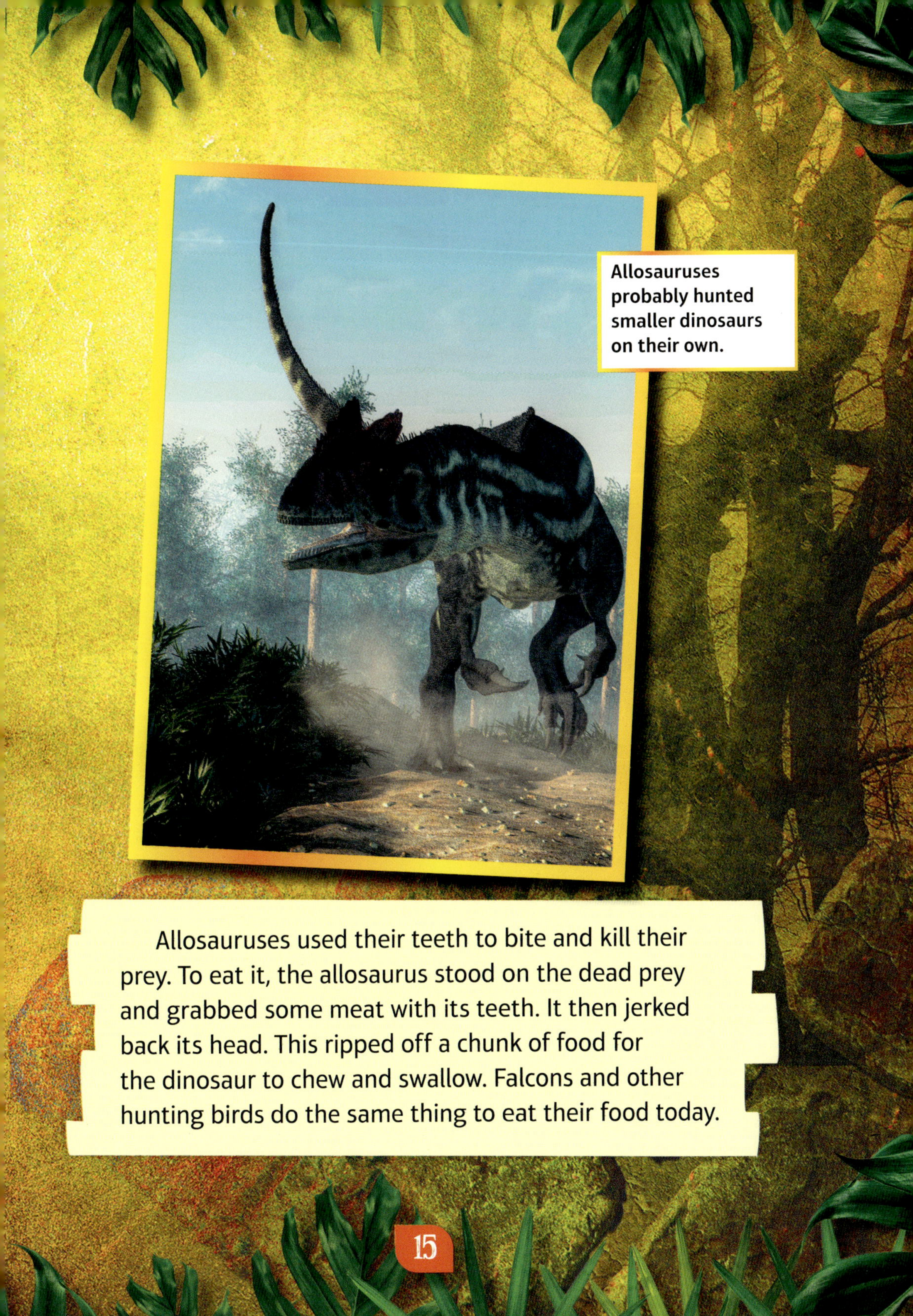

Allosauruses probably hunted smaller dinosaurs on their own.

Allosauruses used their teeth to bite and kill their prey. To eat it, the allosaurus stood on the dead prey and grabbed some meat with its teeth. It then jerked back its head. This ripped off a chunk of food for the dinosaur to chew and swallow. Falcons and other hunting birds do the same thing to eat their food today.

Survival Skills

The two dinosaurs spent their days doing very different things. The allosaurus probably lived in a group, or pack. The pack would hunt together to find and kill food. They then shared the meal. Today, wolves do the same thing. Wolves live and hunt in a pack.

Allosauruses were probably much smarter than stegosauruses. A stegosaurus's brain was about the size of a lime!

A stegosaurus's tall plates would also have given off heat when the dinosaur was too hot.

Dinosaurs would have been too cold to move around much at night and early in the morning. Stegosauruses used the tall plates on their back to catch the warmth of the sunshine as fast as possible. The sunshine heated the blood under the skin. Soon they were warmed up and ready to spend the day eating.

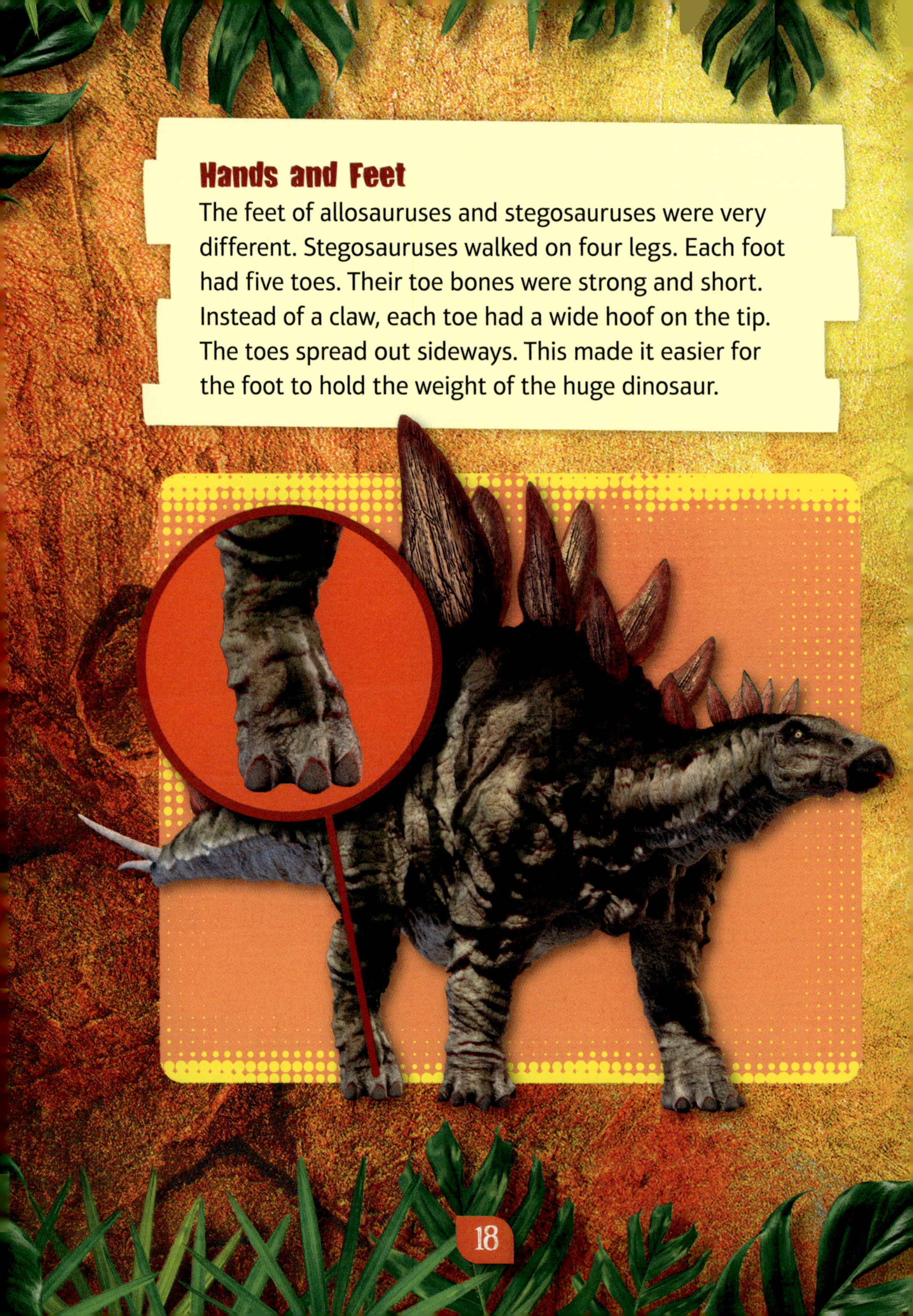

Hands and Feet

The feet of allosauruses and stegosauruses were very different. Stegosauruses walked on four legs. Each foot had five toes. Their toe bones were strong and short. Instead of a claw, each toe had a wide hoof on the tip. The toes spread out sideways. This made it easier for the foot to hold the weight of the huge dinosaur.

Stegosauruses left deep, rounded footprints in the mud. This helps dinosaur experts to figure out how heavy stegosauruses were.

Allosauruses walked on their two back legs. Their hind feet had four main toes, each one with a thick claw for gripping the ground. The dinosaur's hands were much smaller and had only three fingers each. The claws here were very long and sharp to help them grab prey.

Top Speed

In a running race between an allosaurus and a stegosaurus, the winner was always the same. Stegosauruses had a top speed of just 5 miles (8 km) per hour. That is like a fast walk for humans. Allosauruses were much faster. They could run at 21 miles (34 km) per hour.

Stegosauruses traveled long distances, but they moved slowly.

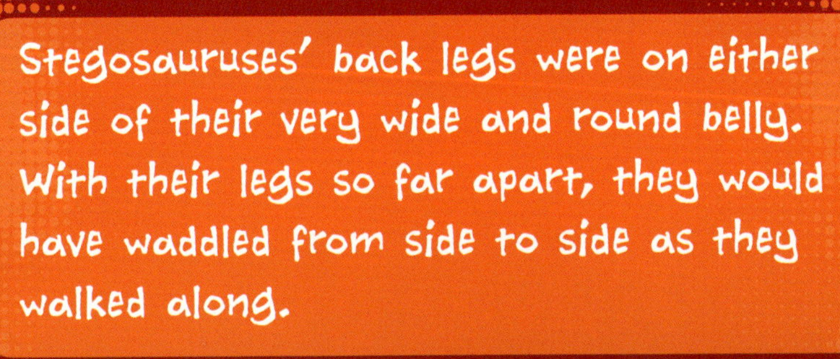

Allosauruses leaned forward as they ran so their back was in line with the ground. The weight of their big head was kept balanced by their long tail. The dinosaur charged at full speed through the bushes to attack their prey.

An allosaurus rushes to attack its prey.

Fighting Skills

Allosauruses could not run fast for very long. Instead of chasing prey, they surprised it in an ambush. During the attack the dinosaur ripped at prey with its hands. It also made many bites. They could eat their prey when it was dead.

Stegosauruses could not run away from attackers. However, their plates protected them from some bites. The stegosaurus's main weapon was the spiked tail. They bashed attackers with this.

The tail of a stegosaurus had four curved spikes made of bone.

Even though they had huge jaws, allosauruses had a weak bite. Their bites were used to make their prey bleed a lot and die quickly.

CHOOSE YOUR WINNER

Two allosauruses have attacked a stegosaurus! One moment the slow plant eater was quietly eating some leaves. Now, two hungry predators are here. The stegosaurus cannot run for it. It is way too slow to get away from an allosaurus. Instead, it is going to have to fight for its life. Its main weapon is its spiked tail. When the allosauruses come near, it swings its tail at them. A good hit would be enough to kill one of the attackers.

The allosauruses are not strong enough to kill the stegosaurus with one bite. Instead they take their time. They slowly wear it down until it is too tired to fight back. The allosauruses are quick, and always on the move. They are keeping away from the stegosaurus's dangerous tail. They take turns rushing forward and biting the stegosaurus.

A baby allosaurus already had teeth when it hatched from its egg. The baby hunted for its own food, catching insects at first.

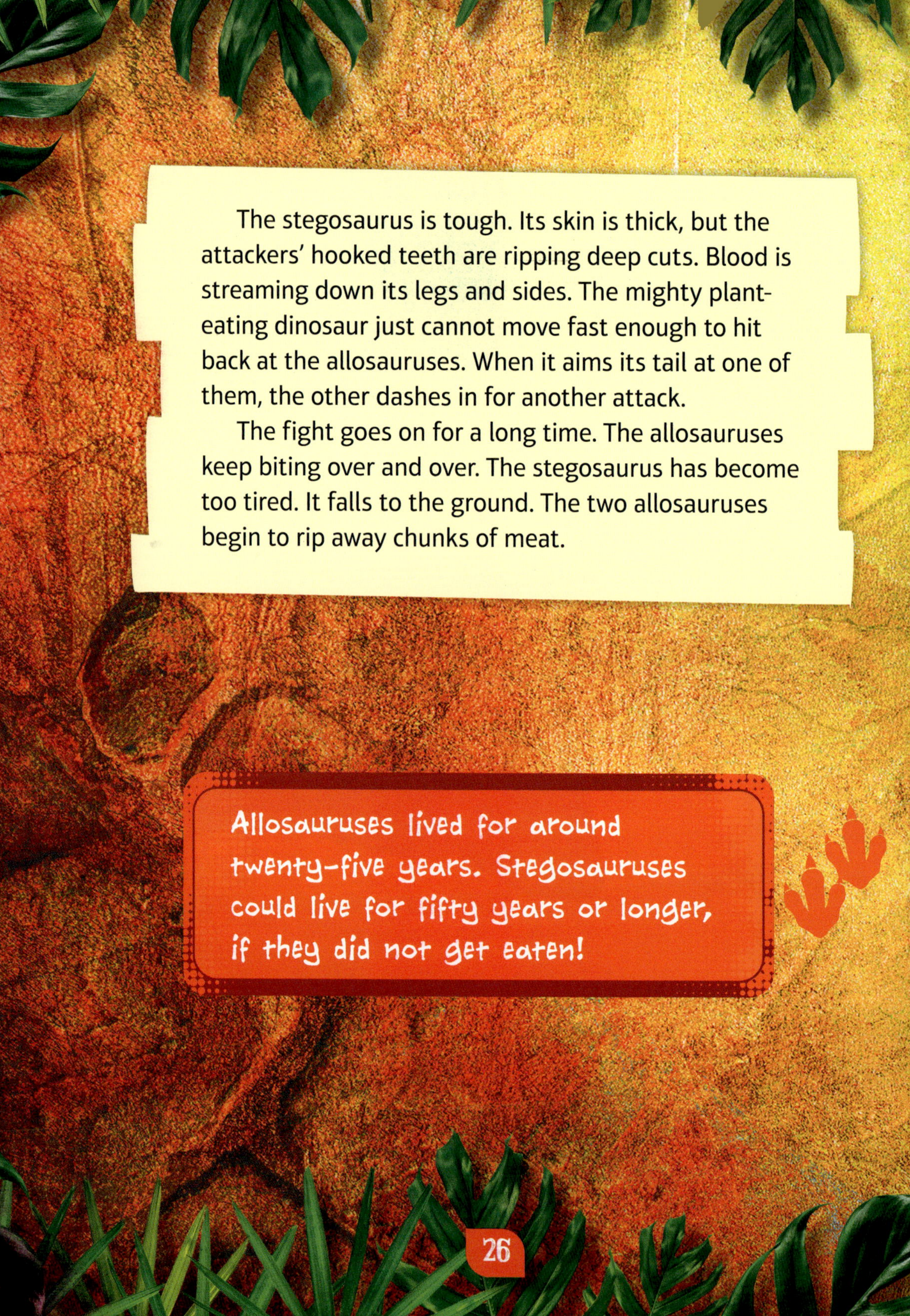

The stegosaurus is tough. Its skin is thick, but the attackers' hooked teeth are ripping deep cuts. Blood is streaming down its legs and sides. The mighty plant-eating dinosaur just cannot move fast enough to hit back at the allosauruses. When it aims its tail at one of them, the other dashes in for another attack.

The fight goes on for a long time. The allosauruses keep biting over and over. The stegosaurus has become too tired. It falls to the ground. The two allosauruses begin to rip away chunks of meat.

Allosauruses lived for around twenty-five years. Stegosauruses could live for fifty years or longer, if they did not get eaten!

The allosauruses are the winner this time! An allosaurus hunting by itself would not attack something as big as a stegosaurus. The next time this pair of allosauruses take on a stegosaurus it could end differently. One good swipe of a stegosaurus's tail could be enough to scare away the hunters.

DINO DUEL

Allosaurus

- Two legs for running fast
- Large jaw
- Long curved teeth
- Sharp claws

Stegosaurus

- A flexible neck
- A spiked tail
- Flat plates along the back to collect warmth
- Swallows stones to grind up food in the stomach

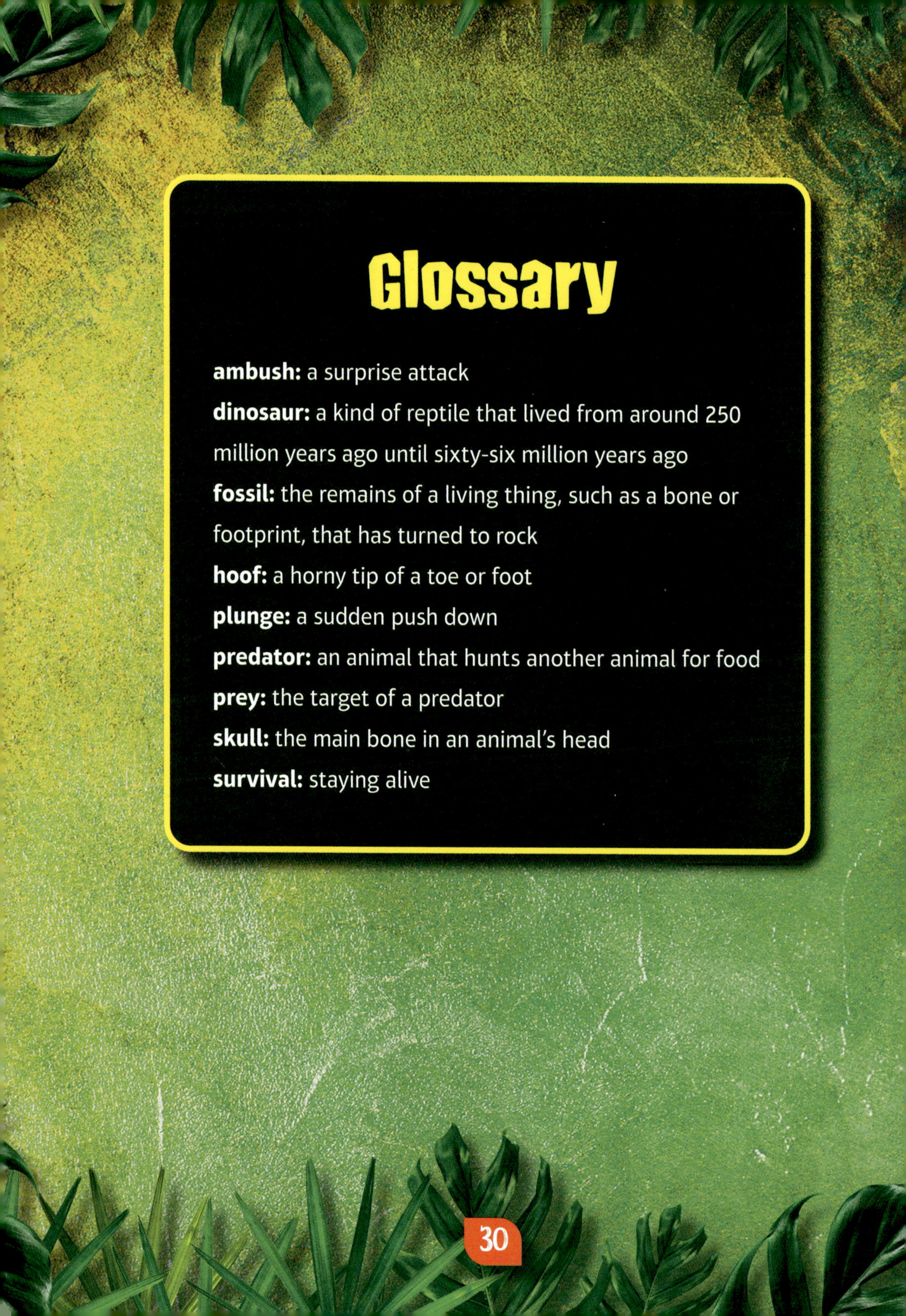

Glossary

ambush: a surprise attack

dinosaur: a kind of reptile that lived from around 250 million years ago until sixty-six million years ago

fossil: the remains of a living thing, such as a bone or footprint, that has turned to rock

hoof: a horny tip of a toe or foot

plunge: a sudden push down

predator: an animal that hunts another animal for food

prey: the target of a predator

skull: the main bone in an animal's head

survival: staying alive

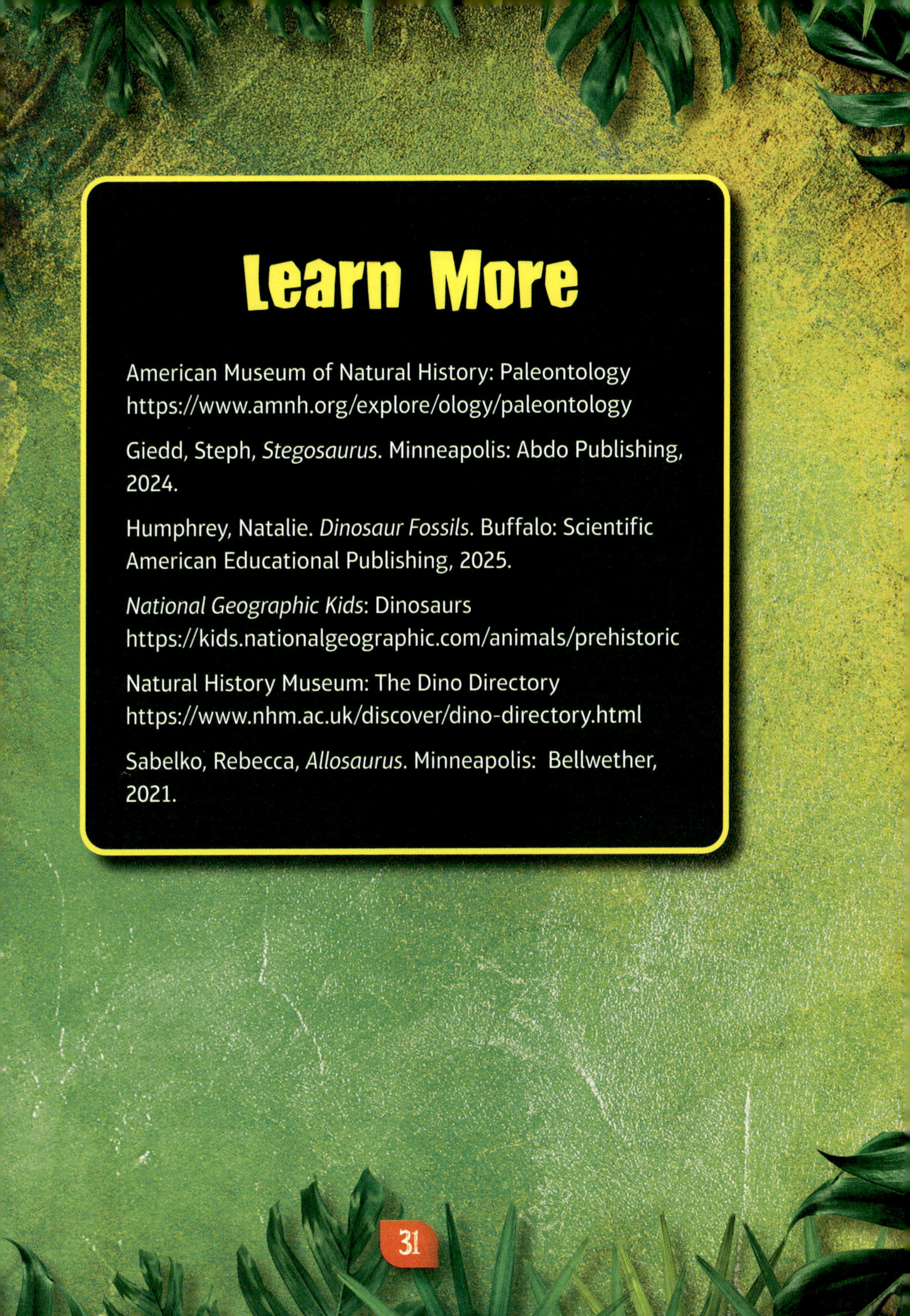

Learn More

American Museum of Natural History: Paleontology
https://www.amnh.org/explore/ology/paleontology

Giedd, Steph, *Stegosaurus*. Minneapolis: Abdo Publishing, 2024.

Humphrey, Natalie. *Dinosaur Fossils*. Buffalo: Scientific American Educational Publishing, 2025.

National Geographic Kids: Dinosaurs
https://kids.nationalgeographic.com/animals/prehistoric

Natural History Museum: The Dino Directory
https://www.nhm.ac.uk/discover/dino-directory.html

Sabelko, Rebecca, *Allosaurus*. Minneapolis: Bellwether, 2021.

Index

Photo Acknowledgments

Image credits: Liidia/Shutterstock, p. 1; Warpaint/Shutterstock, p. 4; Daniel Eskridge/Shutterstock, pp. 5, 14, 15; david.costa.art/Shutterstock, p. 6; Matis 75/Shutterstock, p. 7a; KinoMasterskaya/Dreamstime.com, p. 7b; David Wipf/flickr.com p. 8; Engineer Studio/Shutterstock, p. 9; Sebastian Kaulitzk/Shutterstock, pp. 10, 13, 18; Lefteris Papaulakis/Dreamstime.com, pp. 11, 19, 21b, 28; Noiel/Shutterstock, p. 12; Maria_Gb/Shutterstock, pp. 12–13; Connect Images/Shutterstock, p. 16; Iglwch/Dreamstime.com, p. 17; Michael Rosskothen/Shutterstock, p. 20; e71Lena/Shutterstock, p. 21a; Daniel Eskridge/Dreamstime.com, p. 22; Kitti Kahotong/Dreamstime.com, p. 23; Elenarts/Shutterstock, pp. 24–25; Martin Malchev/Dreamtime.com, p. 27; Mark Turner/Shutterstock, p. 29. Design elements: Kompaniets Taras/Shutterstock; Chaiyapong/Shutterstock.

Cover: Liidia/Shutterstock; Kompaniets Taras/Shutterstock; Chaiyapong/Shutterstock; Connect Images/Shutterstock (top); Mark Turner/Dreamstime.com (bottom).